Gareth's Guide to

BUILDING A SKYSCRAPER

BY RYAN NAGELHOUT

Gareth Stevens
PUBLISHING

Please visit our website, www.garethstevens.com. For a free color catalog of all our high-quality books, call toll free 1-800-542-2595 or fax 1-877-542-2596.

Cataloging-in-Publication Data

Names: Nagelhout, Ryan.
Title: Gareth's guide to building a skyscraper / Ryan Nagelhout.
Description: New York : Gareth Stevens Publishing, 2019. | Series: Gareth guides to an extraordinary life | Includes glossary and index.
Identifiers: LCCN ISBN 9781538220573 (pbk.) | ISBN 9781538220559 (library bound) | ISBN 9781538220580 (ebook)
Subjects: LCSH: Skyscrapers–Juvenile literature. | Skyscrapers–Design and construction–Juvenile literature.
Classification: LCC NA6230.N34 2019 | DDC 720.483–dc23

First Edition

Published in 2019 by
Gareth Stevens Publishing
111 East 14th Street, Suite 349
New York, NY 10003

Copyright © 2019 Gareth Stevens Publishing

Editor: Therese Shea

Photo credits: Cover, p. 1 Funny Solution Studio/Shutterstock.com; cover, pp. 1–32 (background texture) Thiti Saichua/Shutterstock.com; cover, pp. 1–32 (design elements) VDOVINA ELENA/Shutterstock.com; p. 4 Matej Kastelic/Shutterstock.com; p. 5 Romrodphoto/Shutterstock.com; p. 6 courtesy of the Library of Congress/Wikipedia.org; p. 7 Kunal Mehta/Shutterstock.com; p. 9 spyarm/Shutterstock.com; p. 11 Spotmatik Ltd/Shutterstock.com; p. 13 Have a nice day Photo/Shutterstock.com; p. 15 PallavaBagla/Corbis via Getty Images; p. 16 Dave Newman/Shutterstock.com; p. 17 Kyrre Lien/Bloomberg via Getty Images; p. 19 ivvv1975/Shutterstock.com; p. 20 Eugene Lu/Shutterstock.com; p. 21 VICTOR TORRES/Shutterstock.com; p. 22 Naeblys/Shutterstock.com; p. 23 Ron Ellis/Shutterstock.com; p. 25 Richard Joseph/Moment/Getty Images; p. 29 Ammar shaker/Einsamer Schütze/Wikipedia.org.

Printed in the United States of America

CPSIA compliance information: Batch #CS18GS: For further information contact Gareth Stevens, New York, New York at 1-800-542-2595.

CONTENTS

WORDS IN THE GLOSSARY APPEAR IN **BOLD** TYPE THE FIRST TIME THEY ARE USED IN THE TEXT.

UP AND UP

For more than 3,800 years, the tallest building on Earth was Egypt's Great Pyramid of Giza. Its original height is believed to have been about 481 feet (147 m). It was made of more than 2.3 million blocks of stone! To achieve the pyramid's height, the Egyptians made it taper, or get narrower, as it got taller so it remained stable. That's why pyramids have their stepped shape.

Many modern buildings taper, but few look like a pyramid. Today, we have different materials with which to construct and support tall—and extremely tall—structures. Steel and concrete allow us to design and build skyscrapers of great height, creating the stunning skylines you see in large cities. Do you have what it takes to create one of these spectacular buildings? Keep reading and you will!

➤ SPOTLIGHT!

THE GREAT PYRAMID WAS ONCE ABOUT 30 FEET (9 M) TALLER! OVER THOUSANDS OF YEARS, EROSION HAS WORN AWAY THE STONE THE PYRAMID WAS BUILT WITH. IT'S ALSO MISSING ITS TOP PIECE, CALLED THE PYRAMIDION.

Making It Taller

Architects are people who design buildings. Long ago, architects figured out ways to build giant structures before steel and concrete were used. They discovered designs to keep heavy stone walls and roofs from falling down. For example, **medieval** architects constructed buildings with flying buttresses. A flying buttress carries the weight of a heavy structure to the ground. It consists of an arch that extends to a column. Flying buttresses also allowed glass windows to be built into walls.

451 FEET (137 M)
→ height of the Great Pyramid

2,717 FEET (828 M)
→ height of Burj Khalifa, the world's tallest skyscraper (as of 2018)

The Great Pyramid is about 451 feet (137 m) tall today, but skyscrapers are much, much taller. In fact, six Great Pyramids on top of each other wouldn't be as tall as the tallest skyscraper!

INSPIRATION

Are you looking for inspiration for your skyscraper? You might want to tour a city that shows off many designs. Found on the Chicago River and the shores of Lake Michigan, the city of Chicago, Illinois, is filled with skyscrapers! From large, rectangular towers made of glass to **gothic**-style structures made of stone, Chicago's tallest buildings come in all shapes and styles.

Chicago was home to one of the first skyscrapers: the 138-foot (42 m), steel-framed Home Insurance Building, which was built in 1885. Skyscrapers have gotten much taller and taken on different shapes since then, but they've included many advances of the Home Insurance Building, such as safer elevators and modern plumbing. The Home Insurance Building was demolished, or knocked down, in 1931 to make space for another skyscraper.

SPOTLIGHT!
ANCIENT ROMANS USED A KIND OF ELEVATOR AS FAR BACK AS 336 BC!

Home Insurance Building

Elevator Going Up!

One important invention that made skyscrapers possible was the elevator. An elevator has a platform that moves up and down a shaft bringing people to different floors of a building. Different kinds of elevators have existed throughout history. Early elevators were mostly powered by people or animals. A safe mechanical elevator wasn't invented until the 1800s. The first public elevator was **installed** in New York City in 1874. Without elevators, everyone would have to climb many, many stairs!

At just 10 stories, the Home Insurance Building wasn't tall by today's standards. A "story" is another name for a floor of a skyscraper. Stories are measured different ways, so they may be different heights.

GETTING STARTED

It's time to think about money. It costs a lot to build a skyscraper, so it needs to be profitable to make building it worth the effort. That's why every skyscraper starts with a developer. Developers are people who fund real estate deals and oversee the process of building from beginning to end. A successful developer makes sure the skyscraper will be occupied when construction is complete.

Developers often hire an architect to design the skyscraper. They find investors to raise money for its construction. They also work with engineers to make sure the building is safe for its purpose. Developers work with city officials to get plans for a skyscraper approved and then find a team to start building.

$3.9 BILLION

cost of one World Trade Center in New York City

SPOTLIGHT!
DEVELOPERS TAKE BIG CHANCES WHEN THEY FINANCE A SKYSCRAPER. BUT IF IT GETS BUILT, THEY CAN MAKE A LOT OF MONEY!

8

Is It Worth It?

Before a skyscraper is built, studies are done to figure out if the skyscraper is needed and will be fully used. For example, researchers might find out if a section of the city needs more apartments for people to live in or more space for stores. Perhaps the building should hold offices where people can work. The answers these studies find may lead to other questions, such as how big to make the apartments, stores, and offices. Unused space won't make money.

Costly mistakes can be found in a skyscraper's design before it's built.

One World Trade Center

RULES AND REGULATIONS

You must have a plan before starting to build your skyscraper. Even if you draw the coolest-looking building and you have the money to build it, your design has to follow important guidelines. No one wants to step into a building that's in danger of falling down!

Today's skyscrapers follow certain regulations, called building codes. These rules make sure buildings are safe for people's use. A skyscraper needs to be strong enough to hold its massive weight. It also needs to stay standing during windstorms, earthquakes, and other natural **disasters**. Skyscrapers need systems in place to bring water, power, and other resources to people on every floor as well. In addition, equipment must be available to help people get safely out of the structure in case of an emergency.

➡ SPOTLIGHT!

SOME SKYSCRAPERS HAVE POINTS ON TOP WHERE PEOPLE CANNOT GO. THESE ARE CALLED SPIRES. THEY'RE PART OF THE SPECIAL DESIGN OF THE BUILDING.

Tower or Skyscraper?

Some extremely tall structures are called towers. A tower is any building that's taller than it is wide. However, towers aren't built to have people regularly use every floor as skyscrapers are. Instead, elevators bring people up to a few floors, usually at the top of the tower to give people views of surrounding areas. Some examples of towers are the CN Tower in Toronto, Canada, and the Space Needle in Seattle, Washington.

Skyscrapers usually have a similar size as they rise, while towers often have a bigger section on top for people to visit.

Space Needle

RENDERINGS AND BLUEPRINTS

Developers work with architecture and engineering firms to compose a master plan. This is the strategy to guide the building from a drawing to reality. The plan usually includes a timeline detailing when events will occur. It may span a few years from planning to completion.

Artistic drawings from an architect show people what the building will look like on the outside. These are called renderings. However, the actual **specifications** that the building will follow are the blueprints. These drawings are usually white lines on a blue background or blue lines on a white background that detail measurements, materials, and other important features of the structure. They also show where water, power, and other resources will be available throughout the skyscraper.

SPOTLIGHT!

IN PHILADELPHIA, PENNSYLVANIA, ARCHITECTS LONG AGREED NOT TO BUILD SKYSCRAPERS TALLER THAN THE STATUE OF WILLIAM PENN ATOP CITY HALL. ONE LIBERTY PLACE BECAME THE FIRST BUILDING TO BREAK THAT AGREEMENT. OTHERS SOON FOLLOWED.

10

number of skyscrapers taller than City Hall in Philadelphia [as of 2017]

Limiting Skyscrapers

Many cities welcome the building of skyscrapers, but others don't allow them at all. According to the Height of Buildings Act, most new buildings in Washington, DC, can't be taller than 90 feet (27 m) on residential streets, 130 feet (40 m) on commercial streets, and 160 feet (49 m) on a small section of Pennsylvania Avenue. Though some people want to change the rule, it's still in effect today.

Architects, engineers, and developers will continue to meet as a building is being constructed.

DIGGING DOWN AND BUILDING UP

Before a skyscraper goes up, construction workers dig down. Every skyscraper has a sturdy foundation, called a substructure, on which it rests. Steel and concrete are used to secure the skyscraper's substructure to a strong, solid base.

In some places, crews dig through layers of dirt to find solid rock, called bedrock. Holes called footings are then drilled into the rock. Steel beams and concrete are placed in these footings. If the bedrock is too deep to reach, crews drive piles, or vertical supports, into the soft ground and then pour concrete over them to create a firm foundation. The upper portions of a substructure are often stacks of steel beams, called grillage, that rest on a flat concrete pad. The weight of the skyscraper lies on the substructure.

282 FEET (86 M)

depth of piles in the substructure of Shanghai Tower, the world's second-tallest skyscraper (2018)

SPOTLIGHT!

LEONARD JOSEPH OF STRUCTURAL ENGINEERING FIRM THORNTON TOMASETTI SAID: "SHALLOW, STRONG BEDROCK LIKE THAT FOUND IN MANHATTAN IS THE EXCEPTION, NOT THE RULE, IN CITIES AROUND THE WORLD."

Tearing It Down

Some skyscrapers are planned for spaces where buildings are already standing. The old buildings can be demolished in pieces, but bigger buildings are blown up! Special construction crews can do what's called a controlled demolition, which means certain parts of the building are blown up to make it fall in a safe way. The pieces are carried away, and work begins on the substructure for the new building.

Some skyscrapers have places for cars to park underground, but don't worry: The substructure keeping the building strong and safe is deep below this underground section!

The substructure spreads out as a pyramid does to support the massive weight of the structure on top, called the superstructure. The superstructure is usually a **grid** of metal and concrete. Support columns may be found near the outer edges of the building, and a concrete core is found within. Horizontal and **diagonal** beams connect these elements and add extra support. The superstructure acts like the building's skeleton, keeping it upright and concentrating the weight on the foundation.

The outside walls, called curtain walls, usually only support their own weight, not the weight of the interior building. Curtain walls, often composed of pieces called panels, have windows and keep weather out of the building. Commonly, they're anchored to the floors or support columns.

➡ SPOTLIGHT!
WILLIS TOWER (ONCE KNOWN AS SEARS TOWER) IN CHICAGO WAS THE FIRST SKYSCRAPER TO USE THE TUBE STRUCTURAL SYSTEM.

1,450 FEET (442 M)

height of Willis Tower, without its antennae

Totally Tubular

Another load-bearing construction possibility for a skyscraper is a tube structural system. It uses concrete or steel columns connected to beams within a building's outer walls, placing the structure's skeleton on the outside walls. This gives buildings more open floor space inside because there's less need for columns within the center of the building. You can pick out these skyscrapers because they have long vertical steel supports on the outside, with narrow-looking windows between them.

Curtain walls allow skyscrapers to have interesting patterns on the outside, like the exterior of this building in Oslo, Norway.

STEEL AND CONCRETE

There are many kinds of superstructures in the skyscrapers of today, but all are made with concrete and steel. Construction workers use both materials because they have properties that, when used together, make extremely strong structures. At each floor, they carefully place steel rods called **reinforcing** bar, or rebar. They're surrounded by poured concrete to strengthen the assembly. Concrete handles the compression that comes from gravity, while rebar can handle **tension** from weight as well as torsion, or twisting, that the building undergoes due to wind.

Construction workers build the frame of a skyscraper with concrete and rebar one floor at a time, pouring thousands of pounds of concrete and letting it set, or dry, so it becomes strong. As the superstructure rises, so does the skyscraper itself!

SPOTLIGHT!

AS THE SKYSCRAPER GROWS TALLER, THE CRANE IS RAISED HIGHER. WHEN IT'S DONE LIFTING THINGS INTO PLACE, THE CRANE IS REMOVED.

Crane in the Sky

As a liquid, concrete can be pumped up tubes, but other materials for skyscraper construction need to be lifted into place. Skyscrapers use cranes, which are erected right on top of the skyscraper itself, to lift steel and other supplies to workers. The person controlling the crane usually can't see where they're moving things, so other construction workers use radios to tell the crane operator what to do next!

Thousands of construction workers may be needed to work long hours to build a skyscraper.

THE CORE

In the middle of a skyscraper — and the skyscraper's superstructure — is an open concrete column called the building's central core. This space has many key elements of modern living running through it, including power, water, and, just as important, elevators.

You might not have considered it, but elevators are essential to skyscrapers. Super-tall buildings need several elevators, in fact. However, elevator shafts impact the amount of space within a skyscraper for offices and apartments. If a skyscraper doesn't have enough room on each floor, it might not make the developer as much money. But fewer elevators means impatient—and unhappy—**occupants**. Architects and developers have to pick the right number of floors and elevators to make everyone content with the space.

The Shanghai Tower in China has elevators that travel around 40 miles (64 km) per hour! That's twice as fast as those used in most other buildings.

Sky Lobbies

Architects and engineers can limit the number of elevator shafts in high-rise buildings by using express elevators and sky lobbies, or lobbies above the ground floor. Express elevators skip dozens of bottom floors to take people to a sky lobby high above. From there, the people can pick up an elevator that serves only the top floors. This saves time, since people don't have to stop at as many floors.

There is a glass balcony on 103th floor of the Willis Tower in Chicago!

WALLS OF GLASS

As the superstructure goes up, the curtain wall follows it. Curtain walls can be made of many different materials. Since the superstructure is carrying most of the load, a skyscraper's outside walls can even be made of glass! This lets people inside the skyscraper have views of the city from high up.

The style of a building's curtain wall follows a certain design. Some architects make buildings in the same style no matter what city they'll be built in. Others take design cues from the skyscraper's home. In Chicago, for example, 333 Wacker Drive is a blue-green glass building made to match the color of the Chicago River. It curves, so it offers a distinctive reflection of the city's skyline.

Rethinking Glass

Even though glass walls create a stunning effect in skyscrapers, some architects have been turning away from their use in recent years. They think floor-to-ceiling windows allow too much energy to escape in the form of heat in the winter and air conditioning in the summer. Sunlight also easily heats up the building, a problem in hot weather. Architects are looking for new ways for buildings to be **environmentally** friendly.

The architects of this building in London, England, nicknamed the Gherkin, now think the glass walls were a mistake.

FINISHING TOUCHES

A skyscraper's roof might just be another floor that's waterproofed to keep out rain, but many have a spire to add to their artistic appeal. Sometimes spires aren't used for anything, but others have viewing platforms.

There's no need to wait until the whole skyscraper is finished to work on the interior. As each floor is built and enclosed by walls, work can start on the inside. Lighting, plumbing, heating and cooling systems, and electrical, telephone, and internet wiring are just some of the features that finishing crews put in place. Sprinkler systems for fire control are also a must as well as other devices for use during an emergency. A skyscraper might even be "opened" to tenants before it's officially finished.

2,716 FEET (828 M)
→ height of Burj Khalifa

SPOTLIGHT!
SOME PEOPLE THINK IT ISN'T FAIR TO COUNT THE SPIRE WHEN RANKING THE TALLEST BUILDINGS IN THE WORLD. THEY THINK ONLY THE FLOORS IN USE SHOULD BE COUNTED. WHAT DO YOU THINK?

Attractive Additions

All buildings, even skyscrapers, need to be attractive places for people to live and work. People enjoy natural light. That's why the Empire State Building in New York City was designed so people would never be more than 30 feet (9.1 m) away from a window. But views aren't enough. Modern skyscrapers have gardens, pools, fitness centers, movie rooms, and other features to make occupants comfortable.

Nearly 12,000 construction workers were needed to build the Burj Khalifa skyscraper in the city of Dubai in the United Arab Emirates!

FIGHTING FORCES

Even on a calm day, winds can blow more than 100 miles (161 km) per hour at the top of super-tall buildings. The biggest challenge in building a skyscraper is dealing with these and stronger winds. Skyscrapers are actually built to be flexible, or move without breaking. Models of skyscrapers are tested in wind tunnels to see if they can handle strong winds without falling over. Making buildings flexible also braces them against damage from earthquakes and other natural disasters.

Some skyscrapers use more **complicated** systems to battle the wind. A tuned mass damper is an extremely heavy steel or concrete weight at the top of a building. It's connected to the walls by **pistons** and springs. The damper pulls the building back toward its original position whenever high winds blow.

> **SPOTLIGHT!**
> ANOTHER TYPE OF SYSTEM TO COMBAT WIND FORCE IN SKYSCRAPERS USES A HUGE TANK OF WATER TO ADD WEIGHT TO THE TOP OF A BUILDING.

Why So Tall?

Why do people keep building taller and taller buildings? In crowded cities, where there's not much available land, the only space available is up! In addition, skyscrapers are impressive, so companies want to be housed in them and people want to have a home within them. Also, skyscrapers exist to show off **ingenuity** and creativity! However, the higher the building is, the more expensive the cost of construction and tenancy.

The World's Tallest Skyscrapers*

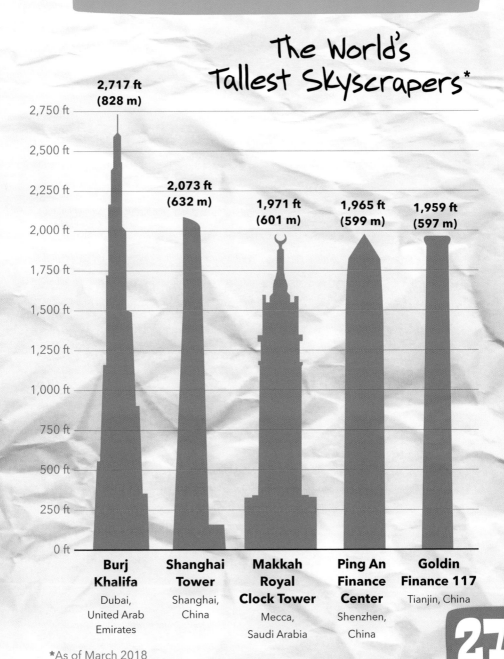

2,717 ft (828 m) — **Burj Khalifa** — Dubai, United Arab Emirates

2,073 ft (632 m) — **Shanghai Tower** — Shanghai, China

1,971 ft (601 m) — **Makkah Royal Clock Tower** — Mecca, Saudi Arabia

1,965 ft (599 m) — **Ping An Finance Center** — Shenzhen, China

1,959 ft (597 m) — **Goldin Finance 117** — Tianjin, China

*As of March 2018

DREAM BIG, DREAM TALL

New kinds of skyscrapers are proposed and built all the time. Some architects want to build an 80-story skyscraper using wood. Another planned skyscraper will use solar and wind power to rotate each floor! Cost, safety, and need will determine if these and others are actually built.

You can be one of the thousands involved in a future skyscraper's construction. Will you be an architect who creates its design? A developer who raises money for its construction and manages its use? Perhaps an engineer who plans and oversees its building? A construction worker who actually builds it? No matter which career you choose, you'll make people look up and marvel at one of humankind's most astonishing creations.

SPOTLIGHT!

THE JEDDAH TOWER IN SAUDI ARABIA IS SCHEDULED TO BE COMPLETED IN 2020. IF ALL GOES ACCORDING TO PLAN, IT WILL BE THE TALLEST SKYSCRAPER YET WITH A HEIGHT OF ABOUT 3,280 FEET (1,000 M)!

Career Course

Whether you want to be an architect, developer, engineer, or construction worker, you'll follow a different career path. You can find out more about what each of these professionals do through research at a library or on the internet. You may be able to start on your path to your career today. For example, if you want to be an engineer, make sure you take lots of science classes and perhaps even join a club for future engineers at school!

TIPS FOR BUILDING A SKYSCRAPER

> Research where a skyscraper will be needed and wanted in a certain area.

> Consult with a developer to raise money for the project and find occupants.

> Have an architect draw up a rendering and blueprints.

> Work with an engineer to decide if the design is appealing and follows building codes.

> Dig and build a substructure.

> Construct the superstructure around the core.

> Decide on a striking curtain wall.

> Make the interior comfortable and impressive.

> Keep building up!

construction of the Jeddah Tower in December 2016

GLOSSARY

complicated: having many steps or parts

diagonal: not going straight across or up and down

disaster: an event that causes much suffering or loss

environmentally: having to do with the conditions that surround someone or something

gothic: relating to a style of architecture that was popular in Europe between the 12th and 16th centuries and that uses pointed arches, tall and thin walls, and large windows

grid: a pattern of lines that cross each other to form squares

ingenuity: skill or cleverness that allows someone to solve problems or invent things

install: to make a machine or a service ready to be used in a certain place

medieval: having to do with the Middle Ages, a time in European history from about 500 to 1500

occupant: a person who is using or living in a particular building, apartment, or room

piston: a piece of machinery that slides up and down in a cylinder

reinforcing: strengthening by the addition of something

specifications: a detailed description of work to be done or materials to be used in a project

tension: the amount that something is stretched

FOR MORE INFORMATION

Books

Bernhardt, Carolyn. *Engineer It! Skyscraper Projects*. Minneapolis, MN: Super Sandcastle, 2018.

Marsico, Katie. *Skyscrapers*. New York, NY: Children's Press, 2016.

McCarthy, Cecilia Pinto. *Engineering One World Trade Center*. Minneapolis, MN: Core Library, 2018.

Websites

How to Build a Skyscraper
scienceworld.ca/blog/how-build-skyscraper
Find out about the essentials of constructing a skyscraper.

Skyscraper Basics
www.pbs.org/wgbh/buildingbig/skyscraper/basics.html
Learn more about the history of skyscrapers and how engineers make tall buildings.

The Skyscraper Challenge
www.pbs.org/wgbh/buildingbig/skyscraper/challenge/index.html
Test your skyscraper-building skills.

INDEX